Adventurous
PUBLISHING

HOW TO BECOME A LEAER?

Published by Adventurous Publishing

Copyright © Paolo Ben Salmi

The author asserts the moral right under the Copyright, Designs and Patents Act 1988 to be identified as the author of this work.

All Rights Reserved. No part of this publication may be reproduced, stored in a retrieval system or transmitted, in any form or by any means without the prior consent of the author, nor be otherwise circulated in any form of binding or cover other than that which it is published and without a similar condition being imposed on the subsequent purchaser.

Copyright © 2022 Paolo Ben Salmi
All rights reserved.

Hardback ISBN: 978-1-913310-35-6
Paperback ISBN: 978-1-913310-59-2

THE BIG QUEST?ON

HOW TO BECOME A LEADER?

THE BIG QUEST?ON

THE BIG QUESTION SERIES IS A BOOK SERIES THAT HAS A MISSION OF HIGHLIGHTING THE WORLDS THOUGHT-PROVOKING QUESTIONS...

WITH

JOHN HAMAN

HOW TO BECOME A LEADER?

IN THIS BOOK WE WILL ANSWER THE BIG QUEST?ON

HOW TO BECOME A LEADER?

INTRODUCTION

HOW TO BECOME A LEADER?

MY NAME IS JOHN HAMAN. I HAD A LONG CAREER IN AIR TRAFFIC CONTROL AT ONE OF THE WORLD'S LARGEST AIRPORTS, SO TO ME, THE TOPIC OF LEADERSHIP IS VERY IMPORTANT.

WE TEND TO THINK OF LEADERS AS BEING HEADS OF COUNTRIES OR BIG CORPORATIONS, OR PERHAPS POLITICAL OFFICIALS OR HIGH-PROFILE PEOPLE. BUT THE FACT IS, WE ARE ALL LEADERS IN OUR OWN RIGHT IN OUR OWN LIVES.

EVERY DAY WE LEAD PEOPLE BY THE INFLUENCE WE HAVE ON THEM, AND SOMETIMES WE DON'T EVEN REALISE IT.

THE BIG QUEST?ON

THERE ARE ALWAYS NEW THINGS TO LEARN ABOUT LEADERSHIP, AND THERE IS ALWAYS ROOM FOR IMPROVEMENT, AND THAT IS WHY WE ARE HERE TODAY; TO TRY TO IMPROVE OUR LEADERSHIP SKILLS.

THE MOST IMPORTANT THING I HAVE LEARNED ABOUT LEADERSHIP IS THAT THE PRIMARY FUNCTION OF A LEADER IS TO BRING OUT THE BEST IN OTHERS. LEADERSHIP IS ABOUT PEOPLE, AND BRINGING THEM TOGETHER AND CREATING HARMONY IS THE BIGGEST CONTRIBUTION GREAT LEADERS MAKE.

GREAT LEADERS DO NOT LEAD TO BENEFIT THEMSELVES, THEY LEAD TO HELP OTHERS, AND THEY ENCOURAGE THEM TO CONTRIBUTE FULLY TO THE WORK BEING DONE. THAT BRINGS OUT THE BEST IN EVERYONE, AND IT HELPS US BE SUCCESSFUL TOGETHER.

BUT THE BIG QUESTION IS, HOW DO WE DO THAT?

HOW TO BECOME A LEADER?

THE BIG QUEST?ON

MY SENSE OF LEADERSHIP HAS ALWAYS BEEN IN ME, AND I THINK IT IS DUE TO MY FATHER'S INFLUENCE. MY FATHER WAS NOT A LEADER, PER SE, BUT HE BELIEVED IN HONESTY, WORKING HARD, SERVING OTHERS, AND STAYING HUMBLE, AND THOSE ARE THE PRIMARY ELEMENTS OF LEADERSHIP.

I THINK I PICKED UP A LOT OF MY FATHER'S INFLUENCE WHEN I WAS GROWING UP, AND THAT IS WHY LEADERSHIP HAS ALWAYS BEEN AN IMPORTANT TOPIC TO ME.

IN MY WORKING LIFE, I DIDN'T REALLY SEARCH FOR LEADERSHIP POSITIONS, THEY ALWAYS SEEMED TO FIND ME, AND PERHAPS THE REASON THEY FOUND ME WAS BECAUSE OF HOW MY FATHER INFLUENCED ME TO THINK AND WORK.

HOW TO BECOME A LEADER?

THE BIG QUEST?ON

IT STARTED WHEN I WAS 20 YEARS OLD. I HAD ABOUT 15 TRUCK DRIVERS WORKING IN MY DEPARTMENT, AND I WAS THE DEPARTMENT HEAD.

THESE GUYS WERE 40 OR 50 YEARS OLD, AND TO THEM, I WAS JUST A YOUNG KID, AND WHAT DID I KNOW?

THE TRUTH IS, I DIDN'T KNOW MUCH, SO FROM THE EARLIEST DAYS OF HAVING A LEADERSHIP POSITION, ONE OF THE LESSONS THAT WERE REINFORCED IN ME WAS "REMAIN HUMBLE," BECAUSE I QUICKLY UNDERSTOOD THAT OTHERS KNEW FAR MORE THAN I DID.

HOW TO BECOME A LEADER?

THE BIG QUEST?ON

OFTENTIMES, THE PEOPLE YOU ARE LEADING KNOW MORE THAN YOU DO, AND THAT'S A GREAT THING.

IT IS GREAT BECAUSE WHEN A LEADER ADMITS THEY DON'T HAVE ALL THE ANSWERS, IT OPENS THE DOOR FOR OTHERS TO CONTRIBUTE THEIR SKILLS AND KNOWLEDGE MORE FREELY, AND THEY USUALLY HAVE MORE TO GIVE THAN YOU REALIZE.

THAT'S HOW GOOD LEADERS BRING OUT THE BEST OF WHAT EVERYONE HAS TO OFFER. WHEN EVERYONE CONTRIBUTES GENEROUSLY, THINGS ALWAYS IMPROVE, BUT TO DO THAT REQUIRES HUMILITY ON THE PART OF THE LEADER.

HOW TO BECOME A LEADER?

"KEEP CALM AND KEEP IT HUMBLE."

THE BIG QUEST?ON

THAT WAS MY FIRST LEADERSHIP POSITION, AND I LEARNED A GREAT DEAL FROM EVERYONE I WORKED WITH. THEN I GOT MY DREAM JOB.

I BEGAN TRAINING TO BECOME AN AIR TRAFFIC CONTROLLER, AND I WAS THRILLED. I ENJOYED MY WORK BECAUSE I LOVED HELPING THE PILOTS AND SERVING THE PASSENGERS ON THE AIRPLANES.

OVER THE YEARS, I GRADUALLY MOVED UP, AND ONE DAY I FOUND MYSELF AS THE AIR TRAFFIC CONTROL MANAGER AT ONE OF THE BUSIEST AIRPORTS IN THE WORLD, AND THAT WAS ANOTHER THRILLING EXPERIENCE FOR ME.

HOW TO BECOME A LEADER?

IT WAS THRILLING TO THINK, "WOW, IT'S NICE TO KNOW THAT PEOPLE TRUST ME TO DO THIS IMPORTANT JOB."

THE FACT THAT PEOPLE PLACED THEIR CONFIDENCE IN ME AS A LEADER WAS MEANINGFUL, AND IT WAS ALSO HUMBLING, AND THAT WAS WHEN I FULLY UNDERSTOOD THE VALUE OF THE HUMILITY THAT WAS INSTILLED IN ME AT A YOUNG AGE.

HUMILITY KEPT ME GROUNDED, I THINK, AND IT MOTIVATED ME TO TRY HARDER TO SERVE THOSE I WAS LEADING.

I AM NOT THE WORLD'S GREATEST LEADER BY ANY MEASURE, BUT I HAVE LEARNED THAT HUMILITY IN ANY JOB IS A BIG PART OF EFFECTIVENESS.

THE BIG QUEST?ON

"LET HUMILITY BE YOUR SUPERABILITY."

HOW TO BECOME A LEADER?

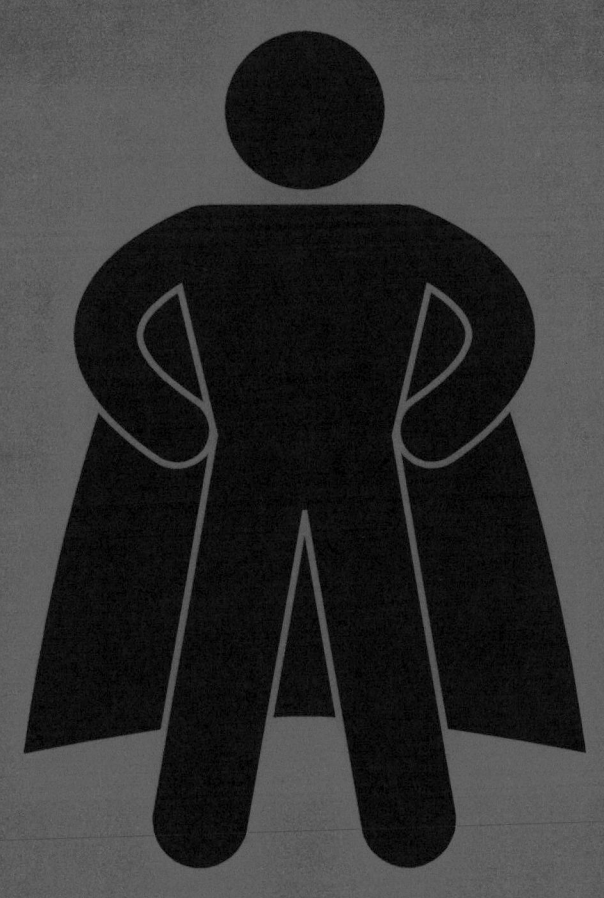

THE BIG QUEST?ON

A LEADER'S JOURNEY:
THE BEGINNING

HOW TO BECOME A LEADER?

THE BIG QUEST?ON

1

"IN ORDER TO BE A GOOD LEADER YOU HAVE TO BECOME A GREAT FOLLOWER."

HOW TO BECOME A LEADER?

I FREQUENTLY DISCUSS THE FACT THAT TO BE A GREAT LEADER, YOU MUST FIRST BE A GREAT FOLLOWER. BUT WHEN I DISCUSS BEING A FOLLOWER, I DON'T MEAN IT IN A DIMINUTIVE SENSE, SUCH AS BEING MINDLESSLY OBEDIENT, OR BEING A ROBOT.

I MEAN BEING A GOOD FOLLOWER IN TERMS OF RESPECTING THE PEOPLE YOU ARE WORKING WITH, BEING COOPERATIVE, AND UNDERSTANDING THAT OTHER PEOPLE HAVE NEEDS TOO.

BEING A GOOD FOLLOWER IS A MAJOR PART OF BEING AN EFFECTIVE LEADER, AND THE WAY TO DO IT IS BY BEING A GOOD COLLEAGUE, A RELIABLE CO-WORKER, AND A LOYAL FRIEND.

THE BIG QUEST?ON

IT IS ALSO IMPORTANT TO RESPECT AND ACKNOWLEDGE THAT OTHERS MAY HAVE DIFFERENT VIEWPOINTS AND OPINIONS ABOUT THINGS, SO IT IS VITAL TO RESPECT OTHER PEOPLE. IF YOU DO NOT RESPECT THEM, THEY WILL NOT RESPECT YOU, AND YOU WILL NOT BE A GOOD FOLLOWER OR AN EFFECTIVE LEADER.

THIS IS WHY I BELIEVE AN IMPORTANT STEP IN BECOMING A LEADER IS TO LEARN TO BE A GOOD FOLLOWER, AND THERE ARE TWO PRIMARY THINGS TO DO:

REMAIN HUMBLE, AND BE RESPECTFUL.

HOW TO BECOME A LEADER?

2
GOOD MORALS AND VALUES.

THE BIG QUEST?ON

THE WORLD IS FULL OF LEADERS.

RIGHT NOW THE WORLD IS STRUGGLING, BUT IT ISN'T STRUGGLING BECAUSE OF A LACK OF LEADERSHIP. I THINK WE ARE STRUGGLING BECAUSE OF A LACK OF <u>EFFECTIVE</u> LEADERSHIP.

WHEN PEOPLE HOLD LEADERSHIP POSITIONS, IT DOESN'T MEAN THEY ARE EFFECTIVE LEADERS. THERE ARE MANY POOR LEADERS IN THE WORLD TOO, AND THAT'S WHAT WE NEED TO GET AWAY FROM.

WE DON'T NEED MORE LEADERS WHO JUST WANT TO GAIN POWER OR GET RICH. WE NEED GOOD AND CARING LEADERS WHO WILL WORK SELFLESSLY TO HELP EVERYONE, NOT JUST THEMSELVES.

HOW TO BECOME A LEADER?

WE NEED THOUGHTFUL LEADERS WHO ARE HONEST AND GENEROUS, AND WHO WILL WORK TO IMPROVE THINGS FOR EVERYONE.

THAT IS FAR MORE WORTHY THAN JUST GETTING RICH.

MAKING THINGS BETTER FOR EVERYONE SO WE CAN ENJOY OUR LIVES AND GET ALONG SHOULD BE THE GOAL, AND GOOD LEADERS DO THAT.

THE BIG QUEST?ON

WHAT I MEAN BY ALL THIS IS THAT LEADERS INFLUENCE OTHER PEOPLE, AND THAT INFLUENCE CAN BE EITHER POSITIVE OR NEGATIVE.

THE WORDS AND ACTIONS OF A LEADER MAY REASSURE PEOPLE, OR THEY MAY MAKE THEM MISERABLE.

THEIR WORDS AND ACTIONS MAY PROVIDE COMFORT, OR THEY MAY CAUSE DISTRESS.

THE INFLUENCE A LEADER HAS DEPENDS ON THE MOTIVATION OF THE LEADER—WHETHER IT IS GENEROUS OR SELFISH—AND THEIR WORDS AND ACTIONS REFLECT THEIR MOTIVES.

HOW TO BECOME A LEADER?

IF THE MOTIVATION OF A LEADER IS TO BE HELPFUL, PEOPLE WILL UNDERSTAND THAT AND THEY WILL RESPOND POSITIVELY.

BUT WHEN THE MOTIVATION OF A LEADER IS GREEDY, PEOPLE WILL SENSE THAT TOO, AND THEY WILL RESPOND NEGATIVELY, AND THAT IS WHERE POOR LEADERSHIP ORIGINATES...FROM SELFISH MOTIVES.

THAT IS WHY LEADERS MUST BE CAUTIOUS ABOUT THEIR MOTIVIVES, BECAUSE THEIR MOTIVES AFFECT HOW THEY TREAT AND INFLUENCE OTHER PEOPLE.

GOOD LEADERS ASK THEMSELVES IF THEY ARE TRYING TO HELP EVERYONE, OR JUST THEMSELVES, AND IF THE ANSWER IS THE LATTER, THEY MAKE CHANGES.

HOW TO BECOME A LEADER?

YOUR INFLUENCE ON OTHERS IS A FUNCTION OF WHAT IS IN YOUR HEART BECAUSE WHATEVER LIVES IN YOUR HEART TENDS TO COME OUT IN YOUR WORDS AND ACTIONS.

THEREFORE, THE MOST SIGNIFICANT OBSERVATION I HAVE MADE OF EFFECTIVE LEADERS IS THAT THEY ARE REALLY GOOD PEOPLE. THEY CARE ABOUT OTHERS AND TRY TO DO WHAT IS RIGHT IN EACH SITUATION.

EFFECTIVE LEADERS DON'T WORRY ABOUT WHAT IS EASIEST OR MOST PROFITABLE FOR THEM. THEY ARE CONCERNED WITH HELPING OTHERS, WHICH IS WHY GOOD CHARACTER IS THE MOST NOTABLE FEATURE OF AN EFFECTIVE LEADER.

HOW TO BECOME A LEADER?

THE JOURNEY OF A LEADER PART 2

THE BIG QUEST?ON

HOW TO BECOME AN EFFECTIVE LEADER

HOW TO BECOME A LEADER?

THEREFORE, IN ORDER TO BECOME AN EFFECTIVE LEADER, YOU MUST DEVELOP WHAT I CALL GOOD "HEART SKILLS."

HEART SKILLS ARE THOSE PERSONAL ATTRIBUTES WE HAVE WITHIN US, SUCH AS HOW CARING, GENEROUS, AND HELPFUL WE ARE.

IN ORDER TO DEVELOP GOOD HEART SKILLS, YOU MUST HAVE AN APPRECIATION FOR PEOPLE.

YOU MUST VALUE THEM, AND QUITE FRANKLY, YOU MUST LOVE THEM.

YOU MUST HONOUR THEM, RESPECT THEM, AND HELP THEM WHENEVER YOU CAN.

THE BIG QUEST?ON

HOW TO BECOME A LEADER?

I ALWAYS SAY, "GOOD LEADERS LEAD PEOPLE TO GOOD PLACES, BUT BAD LEADERS FORCE THEM INTO BAD PLACES."

THIS IS WHY IT IS IMPORTANT TO EXAMINE YOUR MOTIVES AS A LEADER, BECAUSE YOUR MOTIVES DETERMINE YOUR EFFECTIVENESS.

IF THE MOTIVE OF A LEADER IS MERELY TO GET RICH OR TO ACQUIRE MORE POWER, THEY WILL START TO PUSH PEOPLE AROUND AND TREAT THEM AS OBJECTS RATHER THAN PEOPLE.

IN OTHER WORDS, POOR LEADERS TRY TO "MANAGE" PEOPLE IN AN EFFORT TO ACHIEVE THEIR GOALS, BUT PEOPLE DON'T WANT TO BE MANAGED, THEY WANT TO BE WELL LED.

THE BIG QUEST?ON

HOW TO BECOME A LEADER?

EFFECTIVE LEADERS DON'T TRY TO "MANAGE" PEOPLE. PEOPLE ARE PEOPLE, AND THEY ARE NOT OBJECTS OR MACHINES THAT NEED TO BE MANAGED.

BUT PEOPLE DO LIKE GOOD LEADERSHIP, AND WHEN THEY SEE IT, THEY RESPOND VERY POSITIVELY, WHICH IS WHY GOOD LEADERSHIP STARTS FROM THE HEART.

OF COURSE, A GOOD LEADER ALSO NEEDS TO BE KNOWLEDGEABLE AND SKILLFUL, BECAUSE PEOPLE MUST HAVE FAITH THAT THEIR LEADERS KNOW WHAT THEY'RE DOING.

BUT MOST OF ALL, GOOD LEADERSHIP IS A FUNCTION OF GOOD CHARACTER.

THE BIG QUEST?ON

HOW TO BECOME A LEADER?

THE GIFT OF BEING A FOLLOWER.

THE BIG QUEST?ON

THE PREVIOUS SECTION ABOUT THE MOTIVES AND CHARACTER OF GOOD LEADERS ANSWERS THE QUESTION, "WHY IS IT IMPORTANT TO BECOME A GOOD FOLLOWER?"

IT IS ALWAYS HELPFUL TO REMEMBER THE TIMES WHEN YOU WERE "FOLLOWING" OTHER LEADERS-GOOD AND BAD ONES- AND THINK OF THE IMPACT THEY HAD ON YOU. THAT WILL HELP YOU PUT YOURSELF IN OTHER PEOPLES' SHOES, AND YOU WILL UNDERSTAND THE VALUE OF CARING LEADERSHIP.

WHEN YOU ARE A GOOD FOLLOWER, YOU RECOGNIZE THE VALUE OF POSITIVE MOTIVES, AND YOU LEARN TO APPRECIATE THE VALUE OF PEOPLE.

AND AS THE VALUE YOU PLACE ON PEOPLE INCREASES, YOUR LEADERSHIP EFFECTIVENESS INCREASES.

THE BIG QUEST?ON

WHEN THE LEADER'S MOTIVES ARE SELFISH, PEOPLE DETECT THAT, AND THEY GROW SUSPICIOUS, AND THE EFFECTIVENESS OF THE ORGANIZATION SUFFERS.

BUT WHEN THE LEADER HAS A CARING LEADERSHIP STYLE, PEOPLE RESPOND POSITIVELY.

GREAT LEADERS DO NOT LEAD FOR THEIR OWN BENEFIT, THEY LEAD FOR THE BENEFIT OF THEIR COLLEAGUES AND CUSTOMERS.

THEY LEAD TO HELP PEOPLE.

THEY LEAD TO IMPROVING THEIR ORGANISATION.

THEY LEAD TO DO A BETTER JOB FOR THEIR CUSTOMERS.

THEY LEAD TO ADVANCE WORTHY PRINCIPLES AND CAUSES.

HOW TO BECOME A LEADER?

LEADERSHIP IS NOT ABOUT MONEY OR POWER. THINGS LIKE MONEY ARE IMPORTANT, BUT THEY ARE SECONDARY TO THE NEEDS OF PEOPLE.

EFFECTIVE LEADERS TAKE GOOD CARE OF THE PEOPLE THEY ARE LEADING, AND THE PEOPLE TAKE GOOD CARE OF THE COMPANY, AND PROFITS FOLLOW.

PROFIT IS NOT THE MOTIVE OF GOOD LEADERS. SERVICE IS THE MOTIVE, AND PROFIT IS THE OUTCOME FROM DOING A GREAT JOB.

EFFECTIVE LEADERSHIP IS ALWAYS ABOUT A WORTHWHILE CAUSE, AND IT'S ALWAYS ABOUT THE PEOPLE YOU ARE WORKING WITH OR SERVING. THAT IS WHERE EFFECTIVE LEADERSHIP LIVES.

THE BIG QUEST?ON

LEADERSHIP IS NOT ABOUT YOU!

IT'S NEVER ABOUT YOU

HOW TO BECOME A LEADER?

- **SO, YOU MUST FIRST BECOME A GOOD FOLLOWER BEFORE YOU WILL BECOME A GOOD LEADER.**

- **YOU MUST BE A RESPECTFUL PERSON WHO LISTENS QUIETLY AND ENGAGES CALMLY AND HUMBLY IN CONVERSATIONS.**

- **YOU MUST BE WILLING TO ENGAGE IN MEANINGFUL DIALOGUE THAT FOCUSES ON IMPROVING THINGS, NOT ON BEING RIGHT OR GETTING YOUR WAY.**

- **TRY TO BE THE PERSON WHO BRINGS OUT THE BEST IN OTHERS.**

- **REMEMBER THAT GREAT LEADERS DO NOT LEAD TO BENEFIT THEMSELVES, THEY LEAD TO HELP OTHER PEOPLE, AND THEY ENCOURAGE OTHERS TO CONTRUBUTE FREELY.**

HOW TO BECOME A LEADER?

- **BE A CARING PERSON, AND TRY TO DO THE RIGHT THING IN EACH SITUATION.**

- **REMEMBER THAT EFFECTIVE LEADERS POSSESS GOOD CHARACTER.**

- **DO YOUR BEST TO KEEP YOUR MOTIVES HONORABLE, AND KEEP SERVICE AT THE FOREFRONT OF EVERYTHING YOU DO.**

- **AND ABOVE ALL, PRACTICE HUMILITY SO YOU NEVER FORGET ITS IMPORTANCE.**

HOW TO BECOME A LEADER?

- **WHEN YOUR MOTIVES ARE HONORABLE AND YOUR GOAL IS SERVICE, YOUR WORDS AND ACTIONS WILL BE HONORABLE, AND YOU WILL BE AN EFFECTIVE LEADER.**

- **THESE THINGS WILL HELP YOU IN YOUR LEADERSHIP ROLE, AND THE WORLD NEEDS ALL THE GOOD HELP IT CAN GET.**

- **THANK YOU FOR CARING.**

THE BIG QUEST?ON

HOW TO BECOME A LEADER?

"AS A LEADER, YOU ARE NOT ABOVE OTHER PEOPLE, YOU JUST HOLD A DIFFERENT POSITION AMONG EQUALS."

THIS IS A VITAL POINT TO REMEMBER. DON'T RAISE YOURSELF UP ON A PEDESTAL BECAUSE SOMEBODY TITLED YOU A LEADER. YOU ARE STILL JUST A PERSON, LIKE EVERYONE ELSE, SO PLEASE REMAIN HUMBLE.

THE BIG QUEST?ON

HOW TO BECOME A LEADER?

ONE, LAST THOUGHT...

THE BIG QUEST?ON

WE ARE ALL AWARE THAT WE HAVE BIG PROBLEMS IN THE WORLD. WE SEE CRIME, CONFLICT, POVERTY, AND GOVERNMENTS THAT ARE STRUGGLING.

WE HAVE SERIOUS PROBLEMS, AND PERHAPS IT HAS ALWAYS BEEN THAT WAY, BUT THAT DOESN'T MEAN IT HAS TO REMAIN THAT WAY.

SO HERE IS THE BIG QUESTION I WOULD ASK YOU TO PONDER.

HOW TO BECOME A LEADER?

IN THE WORLD TODAY, WE ARE WORKING HARD TO GET MORE FOR OURSELVES, BUT WE DON'T SHOW NEARLY AS MUCH CONCERN FOR THE NEEDS OF OTHER PEOPLE.

WE TEND TO DEFINE OUR SELF-WORTH BY HOW MUCH MONEY WE HAVE, OR BY WHAT OUR POSITION IS, BUT MAYBE THOSE ARE THE WRONG MEASURING STICKS.

PERHAPS WE SHOULD BE ASKING OURSELVES IF WE ARE MAKING A POSITIVE CONTRIBUTION TO THE WORLD. MAYBE THAT WOULD BE A BETTER WAY TO LIVE, AND A BETTER WAY TO MEASURE OUR VALUE.

WE HAVE BIG PROBLEMS THAT WE NEED TO SOLVE, SO PLEASE ALLOW ME TO ASK ONE BIG QUESTION:

THE BIG QUEST?ON.

CAN WE DO BETTER?

THE BIG QUEST?ON.

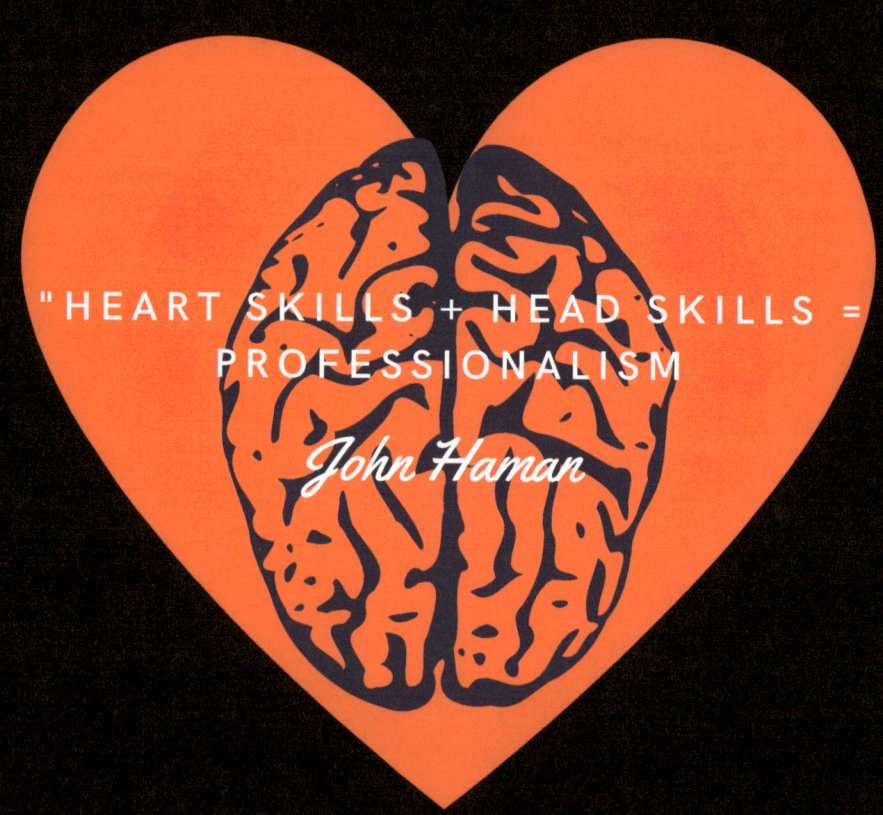

ABOUT *The* AUTHOR
MEET THE MIND
BEHIND THE METHOD

Greetings! My name is John Haman. For the past forty years, I have worked in the air traffic control industry as a controller, manager, mentor, leader, and consultant, but my major interest has always been professionalism.

After decades of experience working with all kinds of people from many different places, I realized the root of many of the world's problems today is a lack of professionalism. I have seen the positive results provided by high-performing professionals, and unfortunately, I have also witnessed the problems created by unprofessional work. Any time professionalism is lacking in a workplace, problems occur, and this is true in every career field. There is no room for unprofessional work because people are counting on us.

Many people possess a limited understanding of words like professional or professionalism, associating them only with specific job titles or qualifications, but professionalism extends beyond your job title. Professionalism is primarily about helping people, regardless of what kind of work you do. Work is not just about earning money. In every job, and especially in high-performance occupations like aviation, there is no room for unprofessional work because the stakes are too high. Our customers expect professionalism, and we owe it to them to deliver.

The biggest thing I learned about professionalism is that it is primarily about serving other people. It involves far more than having a particular skill set; it is about becoming a more complete person. It is about having wide-ranging talents, a generous and caring spirit, and the willingness to use them together to help others. Therefore, a professional is not a "what"—a professional is a "who." What we do at work is insufficient to make us a professional; it is who we are as people that makes us one. Performance, character, leadership skills, and attitude are the necessary ingredients of professionalism.

Great Skills + Great Character = Professionalism.

To address this important topic, I wrote the book WORK HARD AND SERVE OTHERS: IMPROVING OURSELVES AND OUR WORLD THROUGH PROFESSIONALISM.

The book examines the true meaning of professionalism in a series of 51 daily readings. It explains why professionalism is so vital in our workplaces, it provides dozens of real-world examples, and it contains hundreds of ideas about how to improve as a professional, because improving our professionalism is the best hope we have for improving our lives, businesses, governments, organizations, and world.

My work involves writing and teaching others how to increase their level of professionalism, and how to improve their workplaces.

I help professionals develop the "Head Skills" and "Heart Skills" that lead to excellence.

"Work Hard and Serve Others" is available at johnhaman.net or Amazon.com.

LET'S STAY CONNECTED

 Johan Haman

 Work Hard and Serve Others

 www.johnhaman.net

 1johnhaman@gmail.com

""HEART SKILLS + HEAD SKILLS = PROFESSIONALISM"

notes

notes

notes

notes

notes

notes

notes

notes

notes

notes

notes

notes

notes

notes

notes

notes

notes

notes

notes

notes

notes

notes

notes

notes

notes

notes

notes

notes

notes

notes

notes

notes

notes

notes

notes

notes

notes

ABOUT The FOUNDER
MEET THE MIND
BEHIND THE BIG QUEST?ON

AS HEARD ON RADIO & AS SEEN ON TV & IN NEWSPAPERS & MAGAZINES

Websites: https://linktr.ee/AuthorPaolobensalmi

Purpose: To inspire 1 million young people to explore their internal and external world through the teaching of self-discovery, exploration and engineering planting one seed at a time

Paolo is the founder of The BIG QUEST?ON: https://www.linkedin.com/company/89583711/admin

Paolo is a proud ambassador at iamtheCODE and was invited to speak at the UNGA (United Nations Assembly) in September 2021 as a Climate Change activist

Paolo was the youth presenter for World Afro Day 2022: https://www.worldafroday.com/the-big-hair-assembly-2022/

ABOUT *The* FOUNDER
MEET THE MIND
BEHIND THE BIG QUEST?ON

For World Afro Day 2021, over 192,000 children took part in the Little and Big Hair Assemblies from 11 countries. World Afro Day would love to grow this figure to 1 million young people. The Big Hair Assembly is a giant event live-streamed to Secondary #Schools globally and the Little Big Hair Assemblies are hosted by Primary School teachers locally. These events change negative attitudes towards Afro-hair into positive inclusion.

Paolo is a moderator for 10x Kids which is hosted by Sabrina & Scarlett Cardone.

Paolo wrote an article about 'Mindset' in Arabian Business: Could a 'mindset switch' be what the world needs now? - Arabian Business

2021 Paolo was a guest speaker for the UN (United Nations) Global Goals 2030 thanks to I AM The Code founder Lady Marieme Jamme.

LET'S STAY CONNECTED

 Paolo Ben Salmi

 THE BIG QUSET?ON

 @Authorpaolobensalmi

 Info@DreamingBigTogether.Com

"A FLOWER DOESN'T GROW IN A STORM"

www.ingramcontent.com/pod-product-compliance
Lightning Source LLC
Chambersburg PA
CBHW041802160426
43191CB00001B/8